THE TRUTH IS

1. Leveling up your craft to write a story that lives long after you've left the planet is what some might call a ridiculous goal.

2. You will not tell that story after reading just one how-to-write book.

3. You will not tell that story as the result of taking one seminar.

4. You know creating a timeless work of art will require the dedication of a world-class athlete. You will be training your mind with as much ferocity and single-minded purpose as an Olympic gold medal hopeful. That kind of cognitive regimen excites you, but you just haven't found a convincing storytelling dojo to do that work.

5. The path to leveling up your creative craft is a dark and treacherous one. You've been at it a long time, and it often feels like you're wearing three-dimensional horse blinders. More times than you'd like to admit, you're not sure if you're moving north or south or east or west. And the worst part? You can't see anyone else, anywhere, going through what you're going through. You're all alone.

WELCOME TO THE STORY GRID UNIVERSE
HERE'S HOW WE CONTEND WITH THOSE TRUTHS

1. We believe we find meaning in the pursuit of creations that last longer than we do. This is *not* ridiculous. Seizing opportunities and overcoming obstacles as we stretch ourselves to reach for seemingly unreachable creations is transformational. We believe this pursuit is the most valuable and honorable way to spend our time here. Even if—especially if—we never reach our lofty creative goals.

2. Writing just one story isn't going to take us to the top. We're moving from point A to Point A^{5000}. We've got lots of mountains to climb, lots of rivers and oceans to cross, and many deep dark forests to traverse along the way. We need topographic guides, and if they're not available, we'll have to figure out how to write them ourselves.

3. We're drawn to seminars to consume the imparted wisdom of an icon in the arena, but we leave with something far more valuable than the curriculum. We get to meet the universe's other pilgrims and compare notes on the terrain.

4. The Story Grid Universe has a virtual dojo, a university in which to work out and get stronger—a place to stumble, correct mistakes, and stumble again, until the moves become automatic and mesmerizing to outside observers.

5. The Story Grid Universe has a performance space, a publishing house dedicated to leveling up the craft with clear boundaries of progress, and the ancillary reference resources to pack for each project mission. There is an infinite number of paths to where you want to be, with a story that works. Seeing how others have made it down their own yellow-brick roads to release their creations into the timeless creative cosmos will help keep you on the straight and narrow path.

All are welcome—the more, the merrier. But please abide by the golden rule:

Put the work above all else, and trust the process.

THE WRITER'S DAILY PRACTICE

A GUIDE TO BECOMING A LIFELONG
STORYTELLER

DANIELLE KIOWSKI

STORY GRID

STORY GRID

Story Grid Publishing LLC
223 Egremont Plain Road
PMB 191
Egremont, MA 01230

First Story Grid Publishing Paperback Edition
January 2021

For Information about Special Discounts for Bulk
Purchases,
Please visit www.storygridpublishing.com

ISBN: 978-1-64501-061-6
Ebook: 978-1-64501-062-3

For

All Past, Present, and Future Story Nerds

ABOUT THIS BOOK

You're here because you dream of telling a story that works. You want to captivate your readers, to create a story that will stay with them for the rest of their lives, to write a masterwork that will last beyond your lifetime.

Story Grid gives you the tools to do just that. By studying the Story Grid methodology, you can save yourself years of practice and millions of words by grounding your craft in proven technique instead of trial and error.

With Story Grid, your dream is in reach—but Story Grid tools can only make that dream come true if you take them out and build with them. This Story Grid Beat is your blueprint for a daily practice to bridge the gap between theoretical Story principles and practical applications. With the tactics outlined in this guide, you'll build a practice that helps you reach the goals you've set for your writing career—one founded on the core principles of the Story Grid methodology, grounded in the realities of practical application, and fortified to stand up in the writer's struggle against Resistance. Simply put, this is your guide to reach your dreams, one step at a time.

The core of your writing practice will be the Story Grid Rule of 530, our recommendation for a practical daily goal. Every day, you'll write five hundred words of prose and spend thirty minutes doing deep analysis using Story Grid tools. If you're consistent and put in the work, this manageable daily habit will reward you with a steadily growing word count and a deep knowledge of storytelling craft.

In this Story Grid Beat, we'll begin by examining the qualities of a successful daily practice.

Next, we'll delve into the two pillars of the Story Grid Rule of 530 (the 500 and the 30) to explore what makes them indispensable for any writer. We'll go over practical tips and guidelines for putting them into practice, with step-by-step scene planning and a comprehensive overview of the Story Grid analytical toolkit. You'll learn concrete strategies for formulating your personal Masterwork Study Plan that you'll follow in the daily 30 to level up your craft.

Finally, we'll look at how to set up your writing practice to help you succeed. We'll establish a strong foundation with guardrails to keep you on track when you encounter Resistance. You'll learn about the importance of community and how banding together with other story nerds can help you reach your dreams.

Wherever you want your writing career to go, the Story Grid Rule of 530 will help you get there. It all starts with taking the first step in creating your daily practice. Let's get started.

1

THE VALUE OF DAILY PRACTICE

The Story Grid Rule of 530 is a daily practice, meaning you should do your writing and analysis every single day. Sometimes, writers wait to write until they feel inspired by an idea. Let's explore why it's important to write every day—whether or not inspiration strikes.

ESTABLISHING A HABIT

Consistency in your writing practice makes you a writer. The act of showing up transforms you from someone who wants to be a writer into someone who is one, right now. As Steven Pressfield writes in *Turning Pro*, "The difference between an amateur and a professional is in their habits. An amateur has amateur habits. A professional has professional habits."[1] The key point is that a professional is made so by the process, not by the outcome. It doesn't matter how many books you publish or what prizes you win. It matters that you show up. It matters that you dedicate yourself to your craft. This creates your identity as a writer.

Showing up consistently also gives you the best chance of long-term success. When we set out to do creative things, we encounter Resistance. It's inevitable and even welcome because it means we're on the right path. Since we know Resistance will try and stop us, we can make the first move to prepare for its arrival. Before it shows up, while you are excited and hopeful at the start of your practice, build processes that help you to fight Resistance and stay on track. In this Story Grid Beat, we'll look at some tactics to do that—but committing to show up every day is the very first thing you can do to arm yourself for the fight.

It's not enough to wait for motivation to strike you, because that motivation will eventually leave. It will keep you writing for a while, but when you hit a rough patch in the project, Resistance will show up and keep motivation at bay. You'll wait for it to come back while your project sits untouched. If you want to be a writer, you have to put in the work regardless of how you feel. If you show up, day after day, motivation will get the hint and come to you.

Now that we've looked at why daily practice is important, let's identify the qualities that make a daily practice successful.

FOUR FLAVORS OF KNOWLEDGE

If you're reading this book, it's likely you are familiar with the Story Grid methodology and the principles of story outlined in the Story Grid resources. You may have no trouble at all reciting the Five Commandments of Storytelling or explaining how they apply in different units of story. But executing the principles is something else entirely. Even though you use the same knowledge when you apply Story Grid principles in your writing, you use different cognitive pathways when you try to access knowledge for usage instead of recall. A successful daily practice will help you build the pathways to bridge the gap between principle and practice. It will create a robust understanding of Story.

Theoretical study is an important component of learning, but by itself it is not enough to gain true mastery of a subject. Under the "Four-E" model of cognition, four flavors of knowledge contribute to comprehensive understanding. These types of knowledge work together to create true mastery of a concept—in our case, storytelling.

Propositional knowledge is theoretical knowledge. If you have this flavor of knowledge, you understand facts and concepts. You can explain the Story Grid methodology and principles.

Procedural knowledge is the ability to put knowledge into practice.

Perspectival knowledge comes from testing concepts in different environments and contexts. By observing how these concepts work in distinct circumstances, you test the initial proposition and develop a nuanced understanding of how it works in practice.

Participatory knowledge arises when a group of people come together to study and discuss the same concepts. Through conversation in which each participant contributes insights from his or her unique perspective, the group can develop shared knowledge that no one could access alone.

A successful daily practice will develop all four flavors of knowledge to give you a comprehensive understanding of Story and the ability to apply your knowledge in any context.

As we explore the components that make up the Story Grid Rule of 530, you'll see how creating space for this habit in your life will build on your study of storytelling principles. It will round out your knowledge of storytelling by adding procedural, perspectival, and participatory knowledge to the propositional knowledge you get from Story Grid resources. With this comprehensive understanding of Story, you'll be equipped to tell the stories you want to tell.

---

1. Steven Pressfield, *Turning Pro* (Egremont, MA: Black Irish Entertainment, 2012), 20.

2
___

THE 500

In the first part of your daily practice, you'll write five hundred words of prose. If you want to be a writer, it's critical that you get words on the page, whether physical or digital. That's the only way to tell the stories you want to create. It's the only way to get your work into the world.

That's why the first pillar of the Story Grid Rule of 530 centers on word count.

FOCUS ON QUANTITY

Framing this recommendation as a word count goal is no accident. In your writing sessions, you'll be getting a draft done. It might be messy and imperfect. That's okay. The important thing is to write.

By focusing on your word count instead of setting a time limit, you'll produce more work.

If you understand that your output doesn't have to be perfect, you can silence the inner critic that stops your words before they hit the page.

Perfectionism doesn't help you in the writing process. It can work against you by limiting your output and stifling your creativity. In the long run, focusing on producing more will help you to produce better quality stories. How do we know? In the book *Art and Fear*, authors David Bayles and Ted Orland relate the story of Jerry Uelsmann, a professor of photography at the University of Florida. (In the book, the authors altered the details to make it a ceramics class, but the principles remain the same.) The professor split his class into two groups. Students in the first group were told they would be graded on the quality of their best photo while students in the second group would be graded on the number of photos they took. By the end of the class, the best photos submitted by the group aiming for quantity were better than the photos taken with the object of producing a perfect image.

Your writing is like those students' photos. If you get caught up in producing a perfect draft, you'll miss opportunities to practice and improve your craft.

So, when you write your five hundred words every day, embrace the chaos. Get your ideas on the page, messy and imperfect. Once you have a draft, you can edit it. If it stays in your head, there's nothing to edit—nothing to improve. You can only get better if you allow yourself to create something flawed first. As you learn from those mistakes and fix them in subsequent drafts, you'll get better and better until you reach a level of mastery you never could have reached through theoretical study alone.

PROCEDURAL KNOWLEDGE

This process of continual improvement through the editing process works because of the interplay of the flavors of knowledge.

To write stories that work, you need to develop both your theoretical and practical skill sets. The theoretical knowledge of storytelling principles is propositional knowledge. When you put that knowledge into practice, you build up your procedural knowledge. These two modes of knowledge complement and build on each other to form a more comprehensive mastery of Story. The 500 helps you to bring these two modes of storytelling knowledge together.

Once you write your messy, imperfect draft, you have a lump of clay you can mold into something better. You apply your understanding of Story to figure out how you can improve what you've written. As you make those changes, the patterns of a story that works become ingrained in your mind, like muscle memory. The next time around, you'll avoid the mistakes you made last time and find new ways to improve. As the quality of your drafts spirals upward, you hone your writing skills by applying your theoretical knowledge of storytelling. Your procedural knowledge improves through the intentional application of your propositional knowledge.

At the same time, you expand your theoretical knowledge by putting it to the test. When you edit your drafts, you are not only fixing your prose; you're also learning more about the specific concepts in storytelling you need to improve to level up your craft. Further, you apply your abstract knowledge in actual situations where you'll uncover nuances about how the concepts work in different contexts (perspectival knowledge).

As your procedural practice uncovers the areas in your propositional knowledge that need improvement, you'll be able to look for resources to help you focus on those specific areas of your craft. This targeted approach will help you level up your craft more quickly and efficiently than general study, and you'll understand the material more deeply because you'll come to it with an informed perspective from having attempted to put it into practice. You'll connect with the material because you'll understand from experience why it's important.

HOW TO WRITE THE 500

If you already have an established writing practice, it might be easy for you to write five hundred words in a session. But if you dread the thought of staring down a blinking cursor on a blank page, Story Grid can help you overcome that obstacle and start writing.

The key is to plan ahead and break down your writing into tasks you can take on in your writing sessions. If you are looking at a blank page with no idea of what you want to write, the infinite possibilities can prevent you from even starting. Once you have a small, concrete task to accomplish during your writing session, it will be easier for the words to flow.

Focus on the Scene

For your daily practice, focus on writing solid scenes. As Shawn Coyne says, the scene is the fundamental building block of Story. If you can get a scene right, you are well on your way to telling a story that works.

Writing scenes is a great way to practice because you have frequent opportunities to reflect on and assess your progress. The optimal length for a scene is fifteen hundred to two thousand words, so you will complete a scene every three to four days. This means about twice per week, you have the opportunity to review what you've written. This is the time to let your inner editor assess your writing and see if there are any concepts you need to review to make your writing better. It's also a great opportunity to share your writing so feedback from other story nerds can help you to uncover areas to improve.

Plan Ahead

Knowing what you are going to write before you sit down for your daily practice session is critical for getting as much as possible out of your practice. Without direction, you may find yourself staring down a blinking cursor and running out of time. When you have an idea of what you are going to write, you can get started right away.

Story Grid tools come from Shawn Coyne's editing experience, but they can be used for drafting as well as editing. You can use any tools you find helpful to get words on the page, but to prepare for your first practice session, let's look at a simple strategy to plan your first scene.

Plan a Scene

Right now, plan the first scene you'll write during your first Story Grid 530 session. Having a plan in place will make it easier to start writing. You can use Story Grid tools to map out your scene and create your plan.

First, decide on a genre to work in. This will give you the general arena of value shifts that you'll be working with.

Next, choose a type of scene to write. You might choose an Obligatory Moment for your chosen genre (for example, the Hero at the Mercy of the Villain for a Thriller or Lovers Meet for a Love story) or an archetypal scene type that works across genres (for example, Stranger Knocks at the Door or Job Interview).

You might be ready to start writing after deciding on your genre and scene type, or you may want to create an outline of the scene's Five Commandments to follow as you write. Keep in mind that it doesn't have to be very detailed.

You can experiment to find the level of planning that works for you. The important thing is to get to a place where you can sit down for your daily practice and start writing right away.

For now, make sure you have a clear idea of the Inciting Incident and Turning Point for your scene. That will give you enough direction for your first 500 words.

Now that you're ready for your first 500, let's look at the 30 to prepare for the other half of your daily practice.

3

THE 30

After you've written your 500 words, the second part of your daily practice is to spend thirty minutes doing story analysis using Story Grid tools.

Story Grid supercharges your writing craft by helping you to understand the patterns in stories that stand the test of time and by giving you the skills to apply those patterns in your own work. To understand them, you need to see how masterful writers put them into practice. That's why masterwork study is a core component of Story Grid.

When you apply yourself to studying great works, you'll come to understand stories in a way you never have before. You'll understand how the different components of stories work together to create the whole, and you'll appreciate each story not only for its effect on the audience but for the master craftsmanship that went into its creation. You'll build up a breadth and depth of Story knowledge that will give you a library of examples and inspiration at your fingertips.

PERSPECTIVAL KNOWLEDGE

When you can see how Story principles apply across the different works you study, you'll see your propositional knowledge put to the test. By examining how the propositional concepts function in each work, you'll see patterns emerge that will give you insight into the nuances of applying Story Grid principles. You'll deepen your propositional knowledge because you can prove the rigor of a concept by testing it in different contexts. At the same time, your procedural knowledge will grow because each masterwork you study is a model you can use in your own stories.

The perspectival knowledge you develop depends on which perspectives you observe. To build up this knowledge, you'll need a plan for which stories to study and which tools to apply to learn about Story craft. Let's look at how to build your personal Masterwork Study Plan.

BUILDING YOUR STORY LIST

Before you can study masterworks, you need to choose which stories to study. The stories you spend time with will become a part of your internal library. They will nourish your creativity and shape your experience of Story. It's important to choose well.

As you improve your craft, you can adapt your story list and choose masterworks that will improve your storytelling in specific ways. Let's go over a few strategies that can help you build a story list that will allow you to grow as a writer.

Read Widely

One option is to pick stories from across the twelve Story Grid content genres to develop an appreciation for different genres, including ones you might not be familiar with.

Reading stories you would not ordinarily choose will broaden your horizons and challenge the assumptions you have about storytelling. You might find a new favorite genre when you branch out and experience new types of story.

Even if you decide to stay with a familiar genre, reading widely can help your craft.

It can help you understand your chosen

genre through contrast. There are many similarities across genres. Some Conventions and Obligatory Moments, like All is Lost or Hero at the Mercy of the Villain, span multiple genres. Others are closely related to the requirements of other genres. Although the stakes are different, the Big Battle of a War Story and the Big Performance of a Performance Story have a lot in common. By reading widely, you can learn the nuances of these events by comparing how writers implement them in masterworks of different genres. You'll see the subtle differences between the danger to the hero in an Action story and a Thriller story, and once you understand those differences, you can use that knowledge to construct your own stories.

You might even find ways to innovate the Conventions or Obligatory Moments of your genre by taking inspiration from other genres. Adapting ideas and putting them into a different milieu transforms them into something new. Having the vision to remove something from its box and use it in a new way is a creative skill called contextual importing. In *The Last Safe Investment*, Bryan Franklin and Michael Ellsberg write that "contextual importing is responsible for some of the most valuable art, inventions, discoveries, and innovations in history. In some ways it's like creativity's mother, giving birth to a flood of new thoughts and ideas."[1]

Let's look at an example of bringing two concepts together to create something fresh. Imagine that you love medical stories, but you want to innovate on the hospital drama. You read widely, and you discover the masterworks of Crime, like the Sherlock Holmes stories. Something sparks, and you realize that an infection is an invasion—an attack against the body—metaphorically, an inciting crime. From there, it's a matter of applying the Crime genre's Conventions and Obligatory Moments to create a master detective and compelling pursuit of justice in this new environment. That's *House*, a show that captivated audiences because it combined established concepts in an innovative way.

Reading widely establishes a solid foundation of story knowledge and a wealth of inspiration to influence your stories. Once you have that, you can dig deeply into one area that fascinates you.

Read Deeply

It's important to develop a deep understanding of the genre in which you want to write.

Creativity pushes the boundaries of what's

been done before. Like great inventors, you're taking the inventions of your predecessors and tweaking them to come up with something new. To do that, you need to know what already exists.

In addition to becoming familiar with existing stories in your genre, you need to understand existing stories so you can respect the integrity of the structure while refreshing its components. Each Convention and Obligatory Moment has a function in the overall story. It's important to maintain that function as you innovate so you don't break the global story.

In *Silence of the Lambs*, Clarice's Worldview story requires the Convention of a strong mentor figure. The mentor helps the protagonist to challenge his or her existing worldview and prepare for the trials ahead that will test the protagonist's new worldview. Hannibal Lecter is an innovative and interesting mentor because he subverts audience expectations. Instead of guiding Clarice, he manipulates her and makes her confront the darkness in her soul. He lures her into his quid pro quo agreement, which lays bare her secrets and motivations. Though his methods are unconventional, Hannibal still fulfills the core purpose of the mentor. He leads Clarice to question her blind belief in the

FBI and prepares her for the eventual confrontation with Buffalo Bill.

When you read deeply, you can create this kind of innovation by standing on the shoulders of those who came before you. If you ignore the traditions of the genre in which you are writing, you risk "innovating" a cliche or twisting a component of the genre so much that it breaks the global story. When you understand your genre, you can walk the line between these two extremes and create a story that works and brings your readers something new.

When you are compiling a masterwork list with this goal in mind, you'll want to choose several books with similar storylines. By comparing them and seeing what components they have in common, you'll be able to pull out the Conventions and Obligatory Moments of your chosen subgenre and differentiate them from the parts of the story that are unique to each specific masterwork.

Once you understand the rules and requirements of your genre, you'll be able to tell a story that readers of that genre will love because it fulfills their expectations for a great story. You'll also understand the Conventions and Obligatory Moments well enough to innovate them and surprise your readers.

Let Your Work Guide You

The two parts of the Story Grid 530 work together. As you write your prose, you'll discover areas you need to work on to improve your craft. You can use that information to compile a list of masterworks to study that will help you to see how other writers have solved that specific problem. For example, you might struggle with writing a particular scene type, so you could gather a list of works with exemplary instances of that kind of scene.

Masterworks help with more than just the Content leaf of the genre clover, too. If you're writing a short story for the first time, look at short stories to see how other writers have used that form. If you're trying to write a funny book and your humor isn't landing, find comedy in any content genre and study how the writers constructed the jokes so they worked.

What Makes a Masterwork?

There's no definitive list of masterworks. You can find them by reading stories and finding ones that stay with you, by looking for books that have remained popular through time, or by asking for recommendations from friends who love stories. If you ask other Story Gridders, you can specify a certain genre, subgenre, or even story event, and someone will have a recommendation of a story they love that fits exactly what you're looking for.

Story Grid Masterwork Guides are fantastic resources you can use in your own masterwork study. If you choose to analyze a title available from Story Grid, you can compare your own analysis to the editor's. If you do this, there are a couple of things to keep in mind to make sure you get the most value from the exercise. First, don't peek. Once you see an analysis of a work, it will be very difficult for you to see it in another way. Do your analysis independently and compare once you are done. Second, when you compare, don't lose hope if your analysis doesn't match the editor's exactly. This happens. Story Grid is a process, not a set of answers. We all bring our own interpretations to stories. Each masterwork can be many things to many people, and that's part of their beauty. If there are discrepancies between your analysis and the editor's, try to approach it as an opportunity to understand how your thinking differed from the editor's. It may be that you had a misunderstanding, but you might just have had a different (and equally valid) way of looking at the story.

Also, don't be afraid to explore different story forms. Narrative is all around us, in books, films, TV shows, songs, and poems.

That's why this is a Story List rather than a reading list. No matter the medium, the principles of storytelling remain the same. Choose art that speaks to you and see what the analysis can do for your craft.

THE STORY GRID ANALYSIS TOOLKIT

Story Grid offers a wide array of tools you can apply to masterworks in order to learn from them. These different lenses each show you the story in a different way so you can generate insights from what you discover. Generally, the tools fall into two categories. Macro tools enable you to examine the global story to see the overall arc of the work as a whole. Micro tools zoom in to inspect one component of the story—for example, a scene.

Let's review the Story Grid tools you can use in your masterwork study.

The Story Grid Five Commandments

The Story Grid Five Commandments are the core components that every unit of story needs in order to work. They function on both the macro and micro levels, depending on what unit of story you are analyzing.

. . .

The Inciting Incident kicks off the events of the story by knocking your protagonist's life out of balance.

The Turning Point Progressive Complication is the moment when the protagonist's strategy fails, and the character must change in order to be successful.

The Crisis is a dilemma the protagonist faces as a result of the Turning Point. It is a real decision in which the protagonist must give something up, no matter which option he or she chooses.

The Climax is the event in which the protagonist enacts the choice from the Crisis.

The Resolution shows the payoff of the Climax decision.

These concepts are the foundation of the Story Grid methodology, and you will find them embedded in the other Story Grid analytical tools, so it's important you understand them well.

The Story Grid Editor's Six Core Questions

The Story Grid Editor's Six Core Questions are the six questions an editor must answer to understand a story at the global level. While you are doing your 30 minutes of analysis, you are an editor, and these questions are your keys to starting your story analysis. They give you a comprehensive, macro overview of the global story. The questions are:

1. *What's the genre?* To answer this question, evaluate the story using each of the five leaves of the genre clover. For the content genre leaf, examine all the external and internal genres at play, and determine which of these is the Global Genre.

2. *What are the conventions and obligatory moments for that genre?* Identify the Conventions and Obligatory Moments of the Global Genre and explain how the story fulfills each one. The Story Grid Beat *Conventions and Obligatory Moments: The Must-Haves to Meet Audience Expectations* contains more information on the requirements of each content genre.

3. *What's the Point of View?* Identify the point of view, who is telling the story, and what narrative device the story uses. You can learn more about this topic in the Story Grid Beat *Point of View: Why Narrative*

Perspectives Can Make or Break Your Story.

4. *What are the objects of desire?* Describe what the protagonist is trying to achieve. This includes wants, or the external goals the protagonist is trying to attain, and needs, or the internal imbalances the protagonist must correct in order to grow.

5. *What's the controlling idea/theme?* Crystallize the value shift and the protagonist's gift that enables that shift into one sentence that conveys the lesson at the heart of the story.

6. *What is the Beginning Hook, the Middle Build, and Ending Payoff?* Summarize the events of each act of the global story in a sentence each.

The Story Grid Editor's Six Core Questions form the foundation of macro story analysis. Once you have answered them, you can use them to create a Foolscap, which is a one-page summary of the global story.

The Story Grid Heroic Journey 2.0

The Story Grid Heroic Journey 2.0 is a macro lens that builds on the traditions of the

Jungian psychology, Campbell's Hero's Journey, and contemporary cognitive science. To apply this tool, identify the Story Grid Five Commandments to each quadrant of the global story. Next, compare each quadrant's commandments to the structure outlined in the Hero's Journey 2.0 to evaluate how each commandment fulfills the purpose required by the overall structure of the story.

Shawn Coyne has identified the five essential elements of the Heroic Journey 2.0.

1. The Global Inciting Incident is a worldview-destroying unexpected event the protagonist can't really understand.
2. The Global Turning Point Progressive Complication arrives approximately halfway through the story when the protagonist's worldview 1.0 shatters, sending them into utter chaotic confusion.
3. The Global Crisis of the story emerges just after the protagonist realizes that all they held to be true in their past is now lost (the "all-is-lost" moment), from which emerges the mother of all crises, "Should I

keep going, keep trying to find the truth? Or should I quit and surrender to nothingness?"

4. The Global Climax of the story is when the protagonist activates their Crisis choice. They *go on* (a prescriptive heroic journey) or *quit* (a cautionary anti-heroic journey).

5. The Global Resolution of the story is the result of the climactic choice. The prescriptive heroic journey pays off with meaning while the cautionary anti-heroic journey pays off with meaninglessness.

The Story Grid Scene Analysis

The Story Grid Scene Analysis is a micro tool you can use to examine an individual scene. The goal is to determine a scene's story event. To do that, answer these four questions:

1. The Action Story Component: What are the characters literally doing—that is, what are their micro on-the-surface actions?

2. The Worldview Story Component: What is the essential tactic of the characters—that is, what above-the-surface macro behaviors are they

employing that are linked to a universal human value?

3. The Heroic Journey 2.0 Component: What beyond-the-surface universal human values have changed for one or more characters in the scene? Which one of those value changes is most important and should be included in the Story Grid Spreadsheet?

4. The Scene Event Synthesis: What Story Event sums up the scene's on-the-surface actions, essential above-the-surface worldview behavioral tactics, and beyond-the-surface value change? We will enter that event in the Story Grid Spreadsheet.

Story Grid Spreadsheet

Building a spreadsheet is a way to get the micro contents of an entire story into one document. You'll analyze each scene at the micro level, and then put them all together in one sheet so you can see trends or trouble spots. The data you capture in the spreadsheet columns will help you pinpoint any problems. The Story Grid Spreadsheet has fourteen columns. They are:

1. Scene Number
2. Word Count
3. Story Event: This is the description of the Story Event that you generate when you apply the Story Grid Scene Analysis.
4. Turning Point: This is a description of the Turning Point Progressive Complication of the scene.
5. Value Shift: The beginning and ending value states of the scene.
6. Polarity Shift: This is an evaluation of the relative goodness/badness of the value states at the beginning and ending of the scene, expressed in pluses and minuses (+/-, -/+, +/++, or -/- -).
7. Point of View: This identifies who is telling the story in this particular scene.
8. Period/Time: This is the point in time at which the scene occurs.
9. Duration: This is how long the events of the scene take.
10. Location: The setting in which the scene takes place.
11. On-Stage Characters: Characters that are present during the scene.
12. Number: Count the On-Stage Characters.

13. Off-Stage Characters: Characters that are mentioned but do not actually appear in the scene.
14. Number: Count the Off-Stage Characters.

Filling out a spreadsheet will help you to understand a masterwork (or your own story) thoroughly.

To learn more about the Story Grid tools, visit https://storygrid.com/product/story-grid-101/

YOUR MASTERWORK STUDY PLAN

As you can see, there are lots of options when it comes to creating your story list and choosing which levels of analysis to apply to the works on that list. There are millions of possible courses of study. To help you narrow it down, here's a concrete roadmap that will help you to develop your mastery of core story concepts as well as develop expertise in your chosen genre.

Establish the Foundation (Six Months)

The first step in your story analysis plan is to develop a breadth of story knowledge. You'll accomplish this by surveying the Story Grid content genres and sampling masterworks in each one.

The twelve content genres are:

- Action
- War
- Horror
- Crime
- Thriller
- Love
- Performance
- Western/Eastern
- Society
- Status
- Morality
- Worldview

Choose three masterworks in each genre. These can be a mix of books and films depending on your reading speed, the portion of your reading time that you want to devote to masterwork study, and the time that you want to spend on this portion of your study plan. For example, if you want to spend six months on this step (that's our estimated time frame, but it could take more or less time for you), and you read one book per week, you'll have time for about twenty-four books, so you could choose two books and one film for each genre.

As you pick out your masterworks, try to reach beyond your comfort zone by seeking out topics you wouldn't ordinarily be exposed to. Choose works from varying time periods and by writers or directors with varying backgrounds. These strategies will broaden your perspective.

You may find that the content genres of some stories don't match what you expected. This is because marketing categories are not the same as Story Grid genres. This is a common occurrence, and discovering a work's true global genre is part of the analysis process. In the planning stages, just make your best guess. Then, if you discover one that's misclassified, put it in the appropriate bucket and try again to find another masterwork in the genre you thought it was.

After you read or watch each masterwork, spend your 30 minutes of analysis each day applying the Story Grid Editor's Six Core Questions to each work. The Six Core Questions analysis is a great place to start because it teaches you macro storytelling. It's important to get the global story right before you focus on the details of your scenes to avoid wasting words on scenes that don't contribute to your overall story. So it's a good strategy to focus on your macro skills first. It's also relatively quick to apply to a global story, so it allows you to analyze multiple stories and compare them to each other.

You'll be amazed at the insights into story structure you'll gain from this practice and the corresponding improvement to your craft you'll see in your daily 500.

Become a Genre Expert (Three Months)

After you complete your survey of the Story Grid content genres, the next step is to read deeply in your chosen genre. Now that you have sampled a wide range of stories, think about what stories resonate with you the most. That's your genre, or even subgenre. You may find that you are drawn to a specific type of story within a broader content genre.

Choose five masterworks in your chosen (sub)genre. This should be a lot of fun because these are the stories you love.

Analyze each work by answering the Story Grid Editor's Six Core Questions, as you did when you were doing a survey of all the content genres.

Next, pick out the scenes you identified as Obligatory Moments when you were doing your Story Grid Editor's Six Core Questions analysis, and apply the Story Grid Scene

Analysis and Story Grid Five Commandments to each of these scenes.

Once you've done this analysis on each of the masterworks, use a few of your daily practice sessions to review and compare your answers across the genre. Look at the similarities and differences in how each story fulfills the Conventions and Obligatory Moments, and try to understand why the creators made the choices they did.

Deep Dive into a Masterwork (Three Months)

Once you've done the first two steps, you'll have a good understanding of the macro principles of Story. Next, it's time to dive into the micro. Choose a masterwork you love. It's important that you love it because you'll be spending a lot of time with it. It could be one of the five you chose in the previous step, or another masterwork in your chosen genre. (If you do choose a new one, make sure to do the macro steps for it as well.)

In this step, you'll be creating a Story Grid Spreadsheet. Go through your chosen work scene by scene and fill out all fourteen columns in the spreadsheet. Once you've done this, you'll see how the micro components of the work come together to make the global story work. This is an intensive project, but it pays off with a nuanced understanding of how the units of story work together.

Choose Your Own Adventure (Forever)

After you've completed the above plan, you'll have a solid grasp of Story principles and your chosen genre. That doesn't mean your work is done. There's always more to learn about Story, but now it's your turn to write the plan.

Let your own goals and reflections guide you in creating strategies to improve your craft. You may find you want to explore works that have a particular setting or stylistic choice or come from a certain time period. It's up to you. You have all the tools you need to answer any question you have about Story, and you've learned how to use them.

CHOOSE YOUR FIRST MASTERWORK

We've gone over the macro plan for your study of Story, but it starts with one micro step—your first session.

To prepare for your first Story Grid 530 session, choose your first masterwork to analyze. To avoid delaying the start of your daily practice, choose a story you are very familiar with or that you've experienced recently. When you analyze a story, you use the global perspective. If the story has a major revelation at the end that changes the meaning of all the events that came before, you use that information when analyzing the beginning of the work. Because of this, you need to go through each story multiple times: once for the experience, once to get a rough idea of your analysis, and probably a few times after that to answer specific questions that come up. By choosing a story that you already know, you can jump right to the analysis.

If you are already drawn to a story, there's a reason it's compelling to you, and that's a great one to start with.

You might feel overwhelmed because there are just so many stories. If so, you're not alone. It's easy to overthink and try to pick the perfect story to analyze. Don't worry. You'll be analyzing lots of stories over your career. There's no pressure to find just the right one to start. Think about your favorite stories, or the books that are most like the ones you would like to write. Then pick one and jump in.

In your first practice session, you'll be applying the Story Grid Editor's Six Core Questions to this work. It will probably take you several sessions (with some review of the masterwork in between) to complete your analysis, and by the time you're done you'll better understand what makes this story work.

———————————

1. Bryan Franklin and Michael Ellsberg, *The Last Safe Investment* (New York, NY: Penguin Random House, 2016), 109.

4

BUILDING A WRITING PRACTICE

Now that you know what your daily practice will look like, let's go over some concrete tactics for fitting your writing into your day. Any time you start something new, including a new habit, you'll encounter Resistance to implementing the change. Even if you're excited and motivated to start your writing practice, using support strategies to help establish your new practice is critical to making it stick.

SCHEDULE

Days fill up quickly, and even the best intentions to get writing done sometimes get pushed aside to make room for the urgent demands that come up throughout the day. Make your writing practice a priority by scheduling time for it and sticking to your schedule.

The Story Grid 530 will take you about an hour to complete. Try to find a time when you are alert and have energy to devote to your writing and study.

If it's possible, try to schedule your practice for a time when you can run over, if you want to. You may find that you get into a flow state with your writing or analysis and want to keep going past your minimum goal. That's all bonus practice, and it's great to have the flexibility to make that happen.

SET UP YOUR SPACE

Once you know when you'll write and analyze, decide where and how you'll do your practice. What this looks like depends on the space you have available and what makes you comfortable when you write.

Space is crucial for creativity. This applies to both physical and mental space. You need a physical space equipped with what you need to complete your practice. You also need a clear mind that will allow ideas to grow. When you create a consistent physical space in which to do your daily practice, you'll train your mind to open itself up to creativity when you enter that space. That's why it's important to do your practice in one place, as much as possible.

Try to find a relatively quiet place where you're the least likely to get interrupted or distracted. Make sure you're comfortable and can focus. This will help you create the mental space you need to nurture your creativity. Finally, ensure that the physical space can accommodate the tools you need to get your practice done.

GATHER YOUR TOOLS

Next, gather the tools you'll need during your session.

For the 500, you'll need something to write with—whether that's a computer, your phone, or paper and pen. Make sure you can access any programs you are using to write (for example, your word processor) so you don't have any technical problems that interrupt the flow of your practice. If you would like to use dictation instead of typing or writing, set up your microphone and dictation software and test it to make sure it's working correctly.

For the 30, you'll need the masterwork you're analyzing. If it's a film or a song, you'll need a device to play it back while you analyze. You'll also need a document set up in which to do your analysis. Before you sit down for your daily practice, create the format for the analytical tool you're using.

Prepare in advance, as much as possible, so when you sit down to your daily practice, all you need to do is start.

PLAN AHEAD

Planning your session will help you start right away so you can finish your practice in a solid hour of work.

Before your writing session, make sure you have a clear plan for what you will write that day. If you are starting a new scene, refer to the section on planning your scenes to make sure you have a clear idea of where you want your scene to go. If you've already written part of a scene, review it before your session so you'll be ready to jump back in.

For your analysis session, prepare by reading or watching your masterwork and deciding which tool to apply to it. Making that decision will start your subconscious working on the analysis. By the time you sit down to analyze, you'll already have formed some insights into the story.

MEASURE YOUR PROGRESS

After you've completed your practice, celebrate that accomplishment by tracking your progress. Measuring your practice creates accountability. When you can see a record of how many times you've met your goal, you have added incentive to reach it every day.

To stay accountable to yourself, choose a way to track whether you completed your practice goal on a given day. You can use a physical calendar and mark off the days, or you can use an app to track your progress. If you choose an app, you have many options. One benefit is that the developers often use findings from research into habit formation to create apps that motivate you to make progress.

It can also be helpful to connect with other writers who have similar practice goals so you can hold each other accountable. When other people know about your goals and can see your progress, it multiplies your incentive to maintain your consistency. Schedule regular check-ins with your accountability group to let them know how your practice is going. You could even take that opportunity to talk about the stories you're analyzing and creating. Having that support will keep you consistent in your writing practice and excited to keep going.

. . .

These are a few practices you can set up to give your new habit the best chance of success. Ultimately, your commitment to the process will make this work. You are a writer, and writers write. Everything else will follow.

5

FINDING COMMUNITY

When you do your Story Grid 530 practice every day, you'll put your propositional knowledge into practice, developing your procedural and perspectival knowledge to create a deep understanding of Story principles and the ability to apply them effectively. Each day, you'll make steady progress on your study. Imagine what you could achieve if you supercharged that process by multiplying the insights you get from each work and highlighting the areas you need to improve so you can focus your approach.

That's what community can do for you.

At Story Grid, we understand that community has the power to transform your experience as a writer. To help you connect with other writers looking for the same experience, we've created the Story Grid Guild. If you want to take your practice to the next level, joining the Guild can help you do that. When you join, you get access to a vast array of resources, including masterwork analyses and monthly trainings that will help you build up your propositional knowledge. You also get access to a thriving community of writers who are committed to the study of Story.

The Guild is a community full of story nerds, just like you. They, too, understand the Story Grid methodology and believe in the core principles of Story Grid. Yet despite their similarities, their broad range of experiences combine to create a vibrant community of voices.

PARTICIPATORY KNOWLEDGE

Community creates the fourth flavor of knowledge—participatory knowledge. When people with diverse perspectives come together, they create a wealth of insights. Individual contributions play off of each other and challenge each other to create something much greater than any member of the group could have created alone.

Sometimes, groups help you to learn because someone else has a strength in an area you struggle with, and they can help you to understand the concept. This speeds up the learning curve, but it's something that, with time and effort, you could have learned on your own. The participatory knowledge generation process is different, and it's difficult to imagine until you've experienced it.

Participatory knowledge arises through happy coincidences. The circumstances don't seem special. You might be having an ordinary conversation. Then, someone will say something that sparks a thought, and an insight is born. Here's the really interesting part: the person who said something to spark the process probably had no idea it was going to be profound. Each of us has a unique way of expressing thoughts or organizing ideas that seems ordinary to us, but when it layers onto someone else's default way of thinking, it creates a new, revolutionary idea—one that neither person would have seen alone because propositional study doesn't change these patterns of expression. This kind of discovery has to happen in dialogue.

The key to forming a group that can successfully nurture insight creation is shared understanding and a common commitment to improvement. In the Story Grid Guild, everyone shares the Story Grid vocabulary, so they can discuss Story problems easily and clearly. They also share a commitment to Story Grid values and principles. They understand that a story problem is something to be identified and fixed, and it's an opportunity for growth and innovation rather than a personal failing. Writers in the Guild are excited to explore Story ideas together and discover new insights.

The Guild community is a place where writers can count on finding others to share in knowledge creation. The answers and insights you'll get come from members around the world who write in all genres. Their diverse perspectives create the dialogue that multiplies insights and creates participatory knowledge, and in the thriving Guild community, that dialogue is happening every day.

SUPPORT AND ENCOURAGEMENT

The Guild is also a place to find others to share your journey. When you share your goals with a group, you create a support structure that helps you to reach those goals. In the Guild, members help each other stay accountable, but they also understand the Resistance others face and support each other in the struggle to beat it. Together, they can fight Resistance more effectively than they can apart. Many Guild members participate in writing sprints. Just being on a video call with others who are working on writing gives them a sense of connection and purpose, and it gives them an appreciation for the practice of showing up each day.

Sharing their writing journey with others also shifts their perspective. When you see someone else trying to accomplish the same things you are, it can challenge your assumptions. Resistance lies to everyone, but it tells each writer different things to derail the day's creativity. One person might hear that it's impossible to write without absolute quiet; another might hear that silence is deafening and writers need exposure to the friendly chatter of a coffee shop. When you see a community of people, all fighting Resistance and all succeeding and struggling in their own ways, it is easier to see through these lies. How can it be impossible to write in a noisy environment when you see people doing so every day? In turn, you are inspiring them to overcome their own challenges.

The Guild can help you be more productive, but it can also provide support when you are struggling. Sometimes, your creativity will hit a rough patch. It happens to everyone. When you are working alone, that can feel impossible to overcome. You might be critical of yourself for failing. When you're in a group, you see it happen to others. When you see another person struggling, it's easier to see that it's part of the process and offer encouragement instead of criticism. Then, the next time it happens to you, it's easier to take your own advice—or, if not, to listen to the other writers in the group who are there to support you just like you support them. In these ways, the Guild can help you develop not only your writing skills but also your capacity for empathy and compassion. We're often our own harshest critics, but a community can give us the perspective we need to show us our efforts matter.

PERSONAL EMPOWERMENT

Community also creates a space for writers to have a real impact on others. One way to do this is by providing feedback to other writers to help them create something that might not have been possible without your input. In this way, you can contribute to the collective world of Story beyond the stories you create on your own.

You can also implement ideas that will help others in their writing practice. In March 2020, the Guild started hosting writing sprints to give writers a place to come together while they were quarantined at home. Those who attended the sprints found energy, support, and a break from uncertainty when they were with the group. After a while, the officially scheduled sprints ended, and the Guild members took over, taking turns hosting sprints so that they could continue to come together.

The Guild community is a place where you can bring your ideas to life. In the same way the Story Grid tools create a process you can use for your own exploration and insight generation, the Guild creates a platform you can use as a starting point to find others to share in your journey.

MEANINGFUL CONNECTION

The power of community goes beyond writing. In the Guild, writers have found people with whom they share values and goals, and meaningful relationships have developed from this common ground. They've created small study groups that have developed into close-knit groups of friends who share their writing while also sharing a deeper connection. They are bonded by their common struggle against Resistance and their belief in the importance of Story. The shared purpose and values among Guild members creates an environment in which these relationships can flourish.

. . .

Writers in the Guild care about each other, support each other, and challenge each other to improve because of their love of Story and commitment to study. As writers, we're ultimately searching for connection—for our work to reach beyond our limited time and space to touch a reader's heart and change his or her life. In a community like the Story Grid Guild, we can multiply our impact by helping others achieve mastery of their craft, sharing insights, and supporting others on their journeys. Along the way, we can create the kinds of connections that endure for a lifetime.

CONCLUSION

Using the techniques from this Story Grid Beat, you'll be putting words on paper and diving into your masterworks day after day. When you follow the Story Grid Rule of 530, the two pillars of your practice will work together with your theoretical knowledge to build your propositional, procedural, and perspectival knowledge. When you band together with other story nerds who are as committed to studying story and applying the Story Grid methodology as you are, you add the fourth component of participatory knowledge, and all four flavors meld together into a comprehensive mastery of Story.

This is what your daily practice can help you achieve. You'll become conversant with Story principles in a new way. You'll have a breadth and depth of Story knowledge that you can pull from for examples and inspiration.

You'll have the skillset to take that wealth of knowledge and transform it into real results. And you'll have a group of people you share a deep bond with, who are with you every step of the way.

This practice can help you reach your dreams. It has the potential to unlock so much for you, and that can be daunting. Remember, you can do this. Focus on the process. Everything else will follow.

The Story Grid Rule of 530 is intentionally a small, manageable goal to help you achieve consistency. If you show up, day after day, you'll make steady progress toward your goals.

Story Grid makes writing a global story manageable by breaking it down into concrete tasks that give you a clear direction for your writing. Storytelling math breaks down that eighty-thousand-word behemoth into four twenty-thousand-word quadrants and sixty two thousand-word scenes with Five Commandments per scene.

The math works in reverse, too. Five hundred words a day means two scenes per week, and over a hundred scenes in a year. That's almost two novels. Every day, your 500 words are building up your story, and with the craft you learn from your 30 minutes of study, it'll be a story that works.

ABOUT THE AUTHOR

DANIELLE KIOWSKI is a Story Grid Certified Editor based in Las Vegas, Nevada. She grew up with her nose in a book and loves a good story, especially if it's set in a world of urban fantasy or magical realism. As an editor, Danielle is dedicated to empowering ambitious professionals to fulfill their dreams of becoming authors by supporting their development of sustainable and productive writing practices. She believes Story is a fundamental building block of the human experience, and everyone, regardless of their chosen profession, can lead a more meaningful life by engaging with narrative. You can find her online at daniellekiowski.com and writersbynight.com.

ABOUT THE EDITOR

LESLIE WATTS is a Story Grid Certified Editor, writer, and podcaster based in Austin, Texas. She's been writing for as long as she can remember—from her sixth-grade magazine about cats to writing practice while drafting opinions for an appellate court judge. Leslie has written craft-focused articles for the Fundamental Fridays blog and craft books, including *Point of View, Conventions and Obligatory Moments* (with Kimberly Kessler), *What's the Big Idea?* (with Shelley Sperry), and a masterwork analysis guide to Malcolm Gladwell's *The Tipping Point* (with Shelley Sperry). As an editor, Leslie helps fiction and nonfiction clients write epic stories that matter. She believes writers become better storytellers through study and practice, and editors owe a duty of care to help writers with specific and supportive guidance. You can find her online at Writership.com.